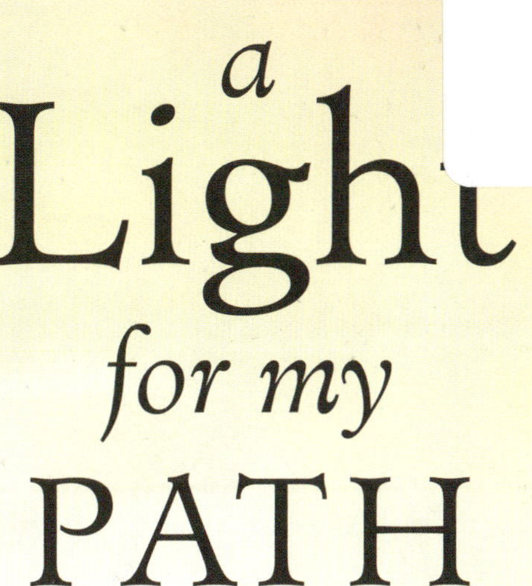

a Light for my PATH

Davis Carman

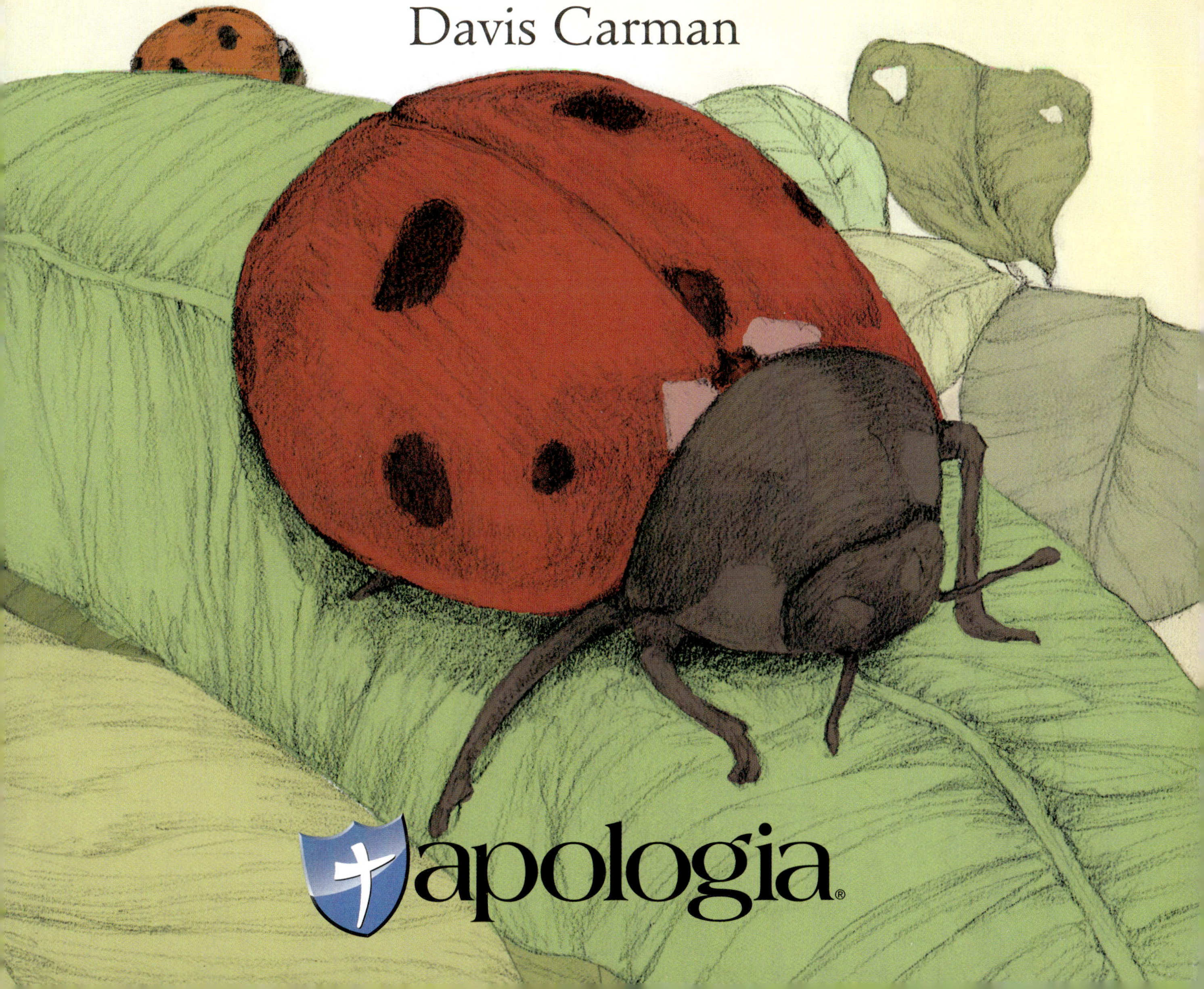

apologia®

A Light for My Path

Published by
Apologia Press,
a division of Apologia Educational Ministries, Inc.
1106 Meridian Plaza, Suite 340/220
Anderson, Indiana 46016
www.apologia.com

Illustrations and Book Design by Alice Ratterree

Manufactured in the USA
Printed by Courier, Inc., Kendallville, Indiana
First Printing: July 2013

ISBN: 978-1-940110-03-5

Dedicated to my children's children,
"the children yet to be born."
(Psalm 78:6)

Introduction

Psalm 119 is a well-known and oft-quoted passage of scripture that's usually noted for being the longest chapter in the Bible. This psalm is the prayer of a person who delights in and lives by every word that proceeds from the mouth of God. In it the author has much to say about God's Word, law, statutes, decrees, commands, and precepts, describing them as comforting, eternal, perfect, and true.

This is a Psalm to read, know, and love at an early age. Adults and children through the centuries have memorized many of the words contained in this psalm:

"I have hidden your word in my heart that I might not sin against you."

"Your commands make me wiser than my enemies."

"You are my refuge and my shield; I have put my hope in your word."

The title of the book you hold in your hands is taken from Psalm 119:105, "Your word is a lamp to my feet and a light for my path."

The purpose of this book is fourfold. First, the book is meant to be read by parent and child while snuggling together on the couch, or while tucking the child into bed at night. Reading together is a great way for you to bond with your young blessings, and I hope this book will provide you and your children some wonderful memories of reading time spent together.

Second, this book is designed to help your child learn the letters of the English alphabet. Each page provides an illustration of God's magnificent creation, with a central image of an animal or plant that begins with the featured letter for that page. For example, the *D* page is illustrated with dandelions, the *E* page has a picture of an elephant, and the *F* page shows a flamingo. Notice that the words *dandelion, elephant,* and *flamingo* do not appear on these pages. Only the artist's rendering of this animal or plant is shown to reinforce that God is the Creator of all things. You may also notice that the creature or plant representing the previous letter is also visible, but often in a smaller size. Thus, there's a subtle spray of dandelions on the *E* page, while some elephants appear in the distance on the *F* page where the flamingo is the featured animal. This theme continues through the *Z* page, where your child will see a yak (from the *Y* page) in the distance with a zebra in the foreground. On this page, the alphabet comes full circle, as the zebra is eyeing the ant from the *A* page.

An important element of children learning their ABCs is to understand that each letter has a capital and lowercase form. On each page the child will easily identify the capital letter as it is large and stands alone. The text found directly under or alongside the large capital letter starts with a lowercase version of the same letter. Be sure you take time to point out to your young child that this is the same letter written a different way, since every letter can be written two ways. (The only exception to this rule is the letter *x*. It was hard enough finding something in God's creation that begins with an *x*, and I was unable to find a word beginning with *x* that describes God's Word. So I chose to go with excellent because its first syllable makes the sound of an *x* and the word includes a lowercase *x* when spelled out.)

Most importantly, this book is meant to instill in children a love and reverence, or deep respect, for God's Word, thereby giving children a sincere desire to read the Bible and learn what it has to say. For each letter of the alphabet, I have identified a specific word describing an attribute of God's Word. For example, the *T* page says that God's Word, law, statutes, decrees, commands, and precepts are *True*, while the *U* page uses the word *Universal* as the description. These words, combined with the simple repetition within the pages, will help your child hear, read, and know God's written words and, consequently, fall in love with the living Word, God's only Son, Jesus Christ.

The following list will help you identify the plant or animal we've used to correspond to each letter in the alphabet. This list also acts as a quick reference to the words I've used to describe God's Word, law, statutes, decrees, commands, and precepts:

A	Absolute	Ant
B	Blessings	Butterfly
C	Comforting	Caterpillar
D	Delightful	Dandelion
E	Eternal	Elephant
F	Faithful	Flamingo
G	Good	Giraffe
H	Helpful	Hippopotamus
I	Instructive	Iguana
J	Just	Jellyfish
K	Kind	Koala
L	Light	Ladybug
M	Merciful	Mouse
N	Near	Narwal
O	Orderly	Otter
P	Perfect	Peacock
Q	Quieting	Quail
R	Righteous	Rabbit
S	Steadfast	Swan
T	True	Turtle
U	Universal	Urchin (sea)
V	Valuable	Vine (grape)
W	Wonderful	Whale
X	eXcellent	Xantus's hummingbird
Y	Year-round	Yak
Z	The A and the Z	Zebra

Finally, you can use this book to teach your child the Hebrew alphabet. Psalm 119 is an acrostic poem, a literary composition in which the writer uses the letters of a word or alphabet as the initial letters for a series of lines or stanzas. This particular poem is divided into twenty-two stanzas, one for each letter in the Hebrew alphabet. The twenty-two stanzas of Psalm 119 occupy the last twenty-two pages of the book. The corresponding Hebrew letter for each stanza is shown at the top of the page along with its English spelling to help you pronounce the letter correctly. This is an optional learning tool, but a potentially influential one. Because the Old Testament was written primarily in Hebrew, knowing the Hebrew alphabet might give your children a connection with God's Word that draws their hearts and minds to better learn and know its vital message.

Davis —

Davis Carman

God's Word, Law, Statutes, Decrees, Commands, and Precepts are

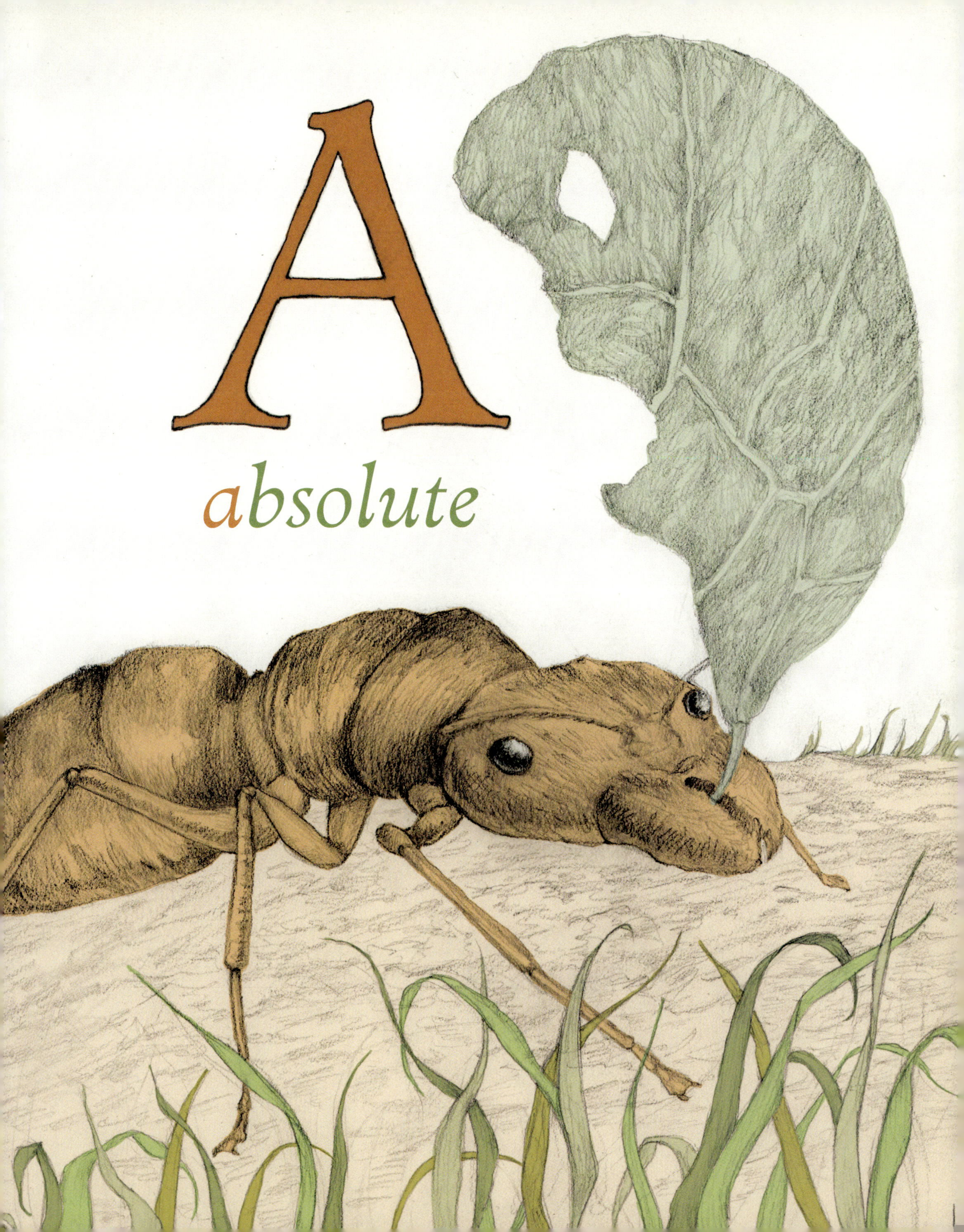
A
absolute

God's Word, Law, Statutes, Decrees, Commands, and Precepts are

B
blessings

God's Word, Law, Statutes, Decrees, Commands, and Precepts are

C

comforting

God's Word, Law, Statutes, Decrees, Commands, and Precepts are

D
delightful

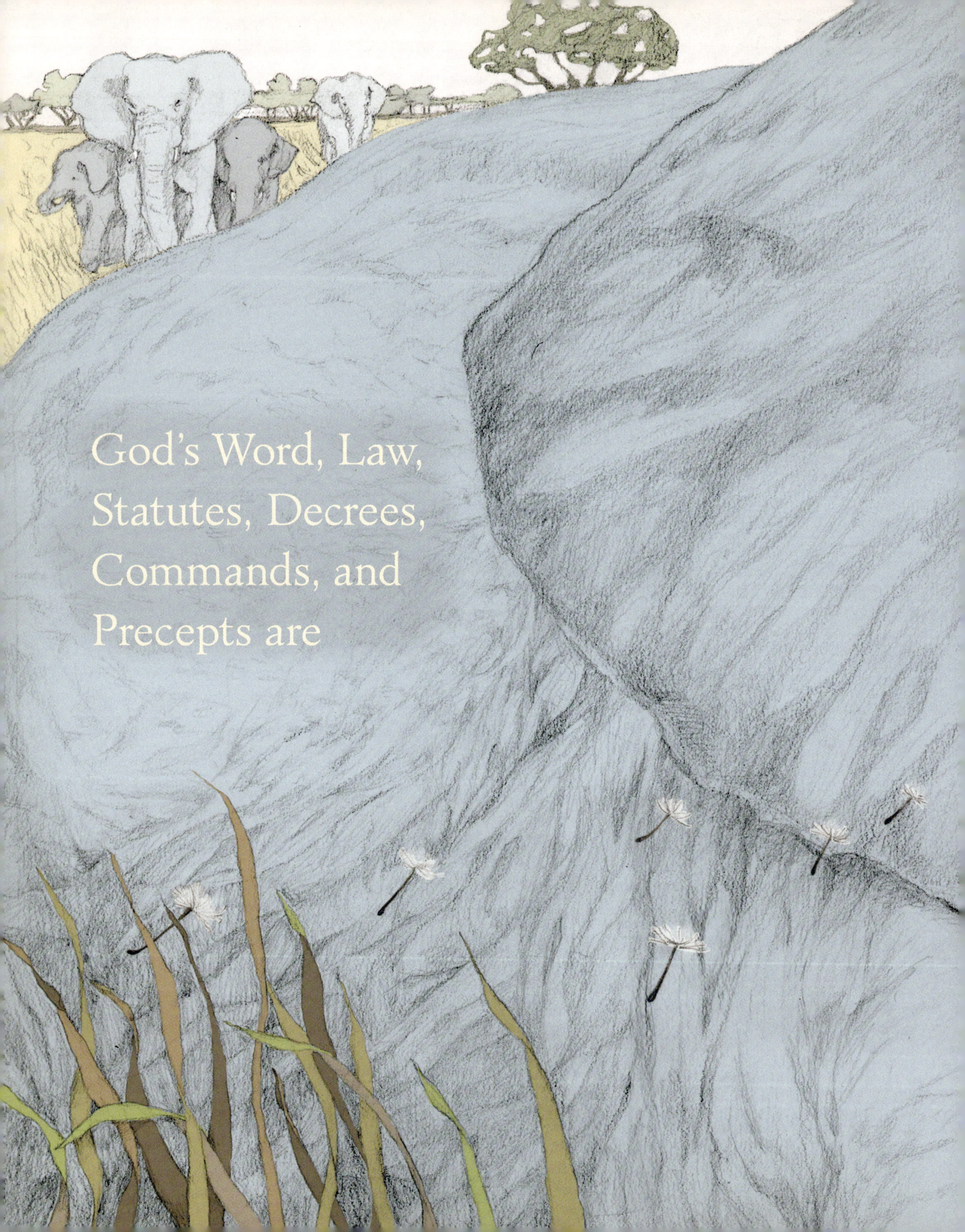

God's Word, Law, Statutes, Decrees, Commands, and Precepts are

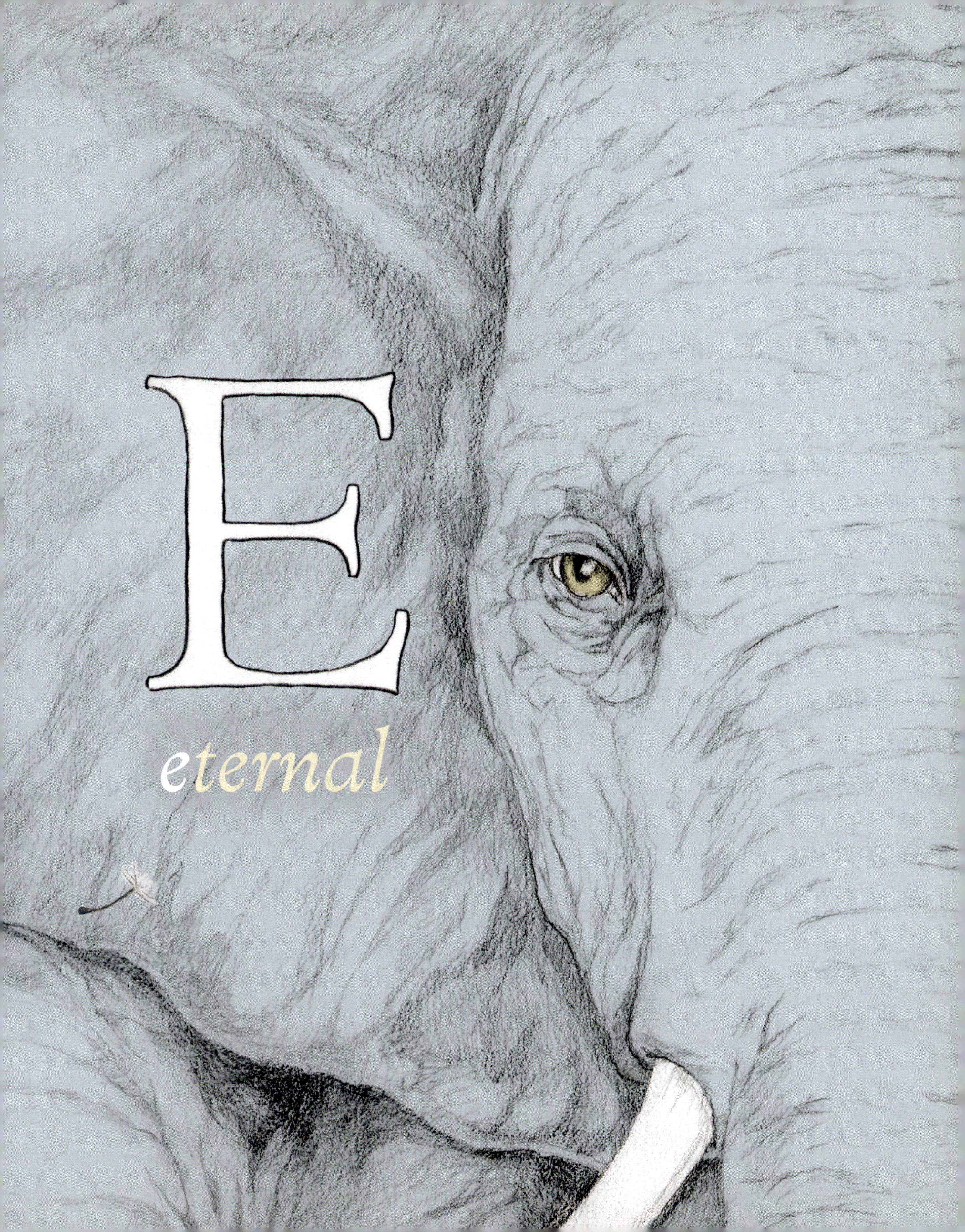
E
eternal

God's Word,
Law,
Statutes,
Decrees,
Commands,
and
Precepts are

F
faithful

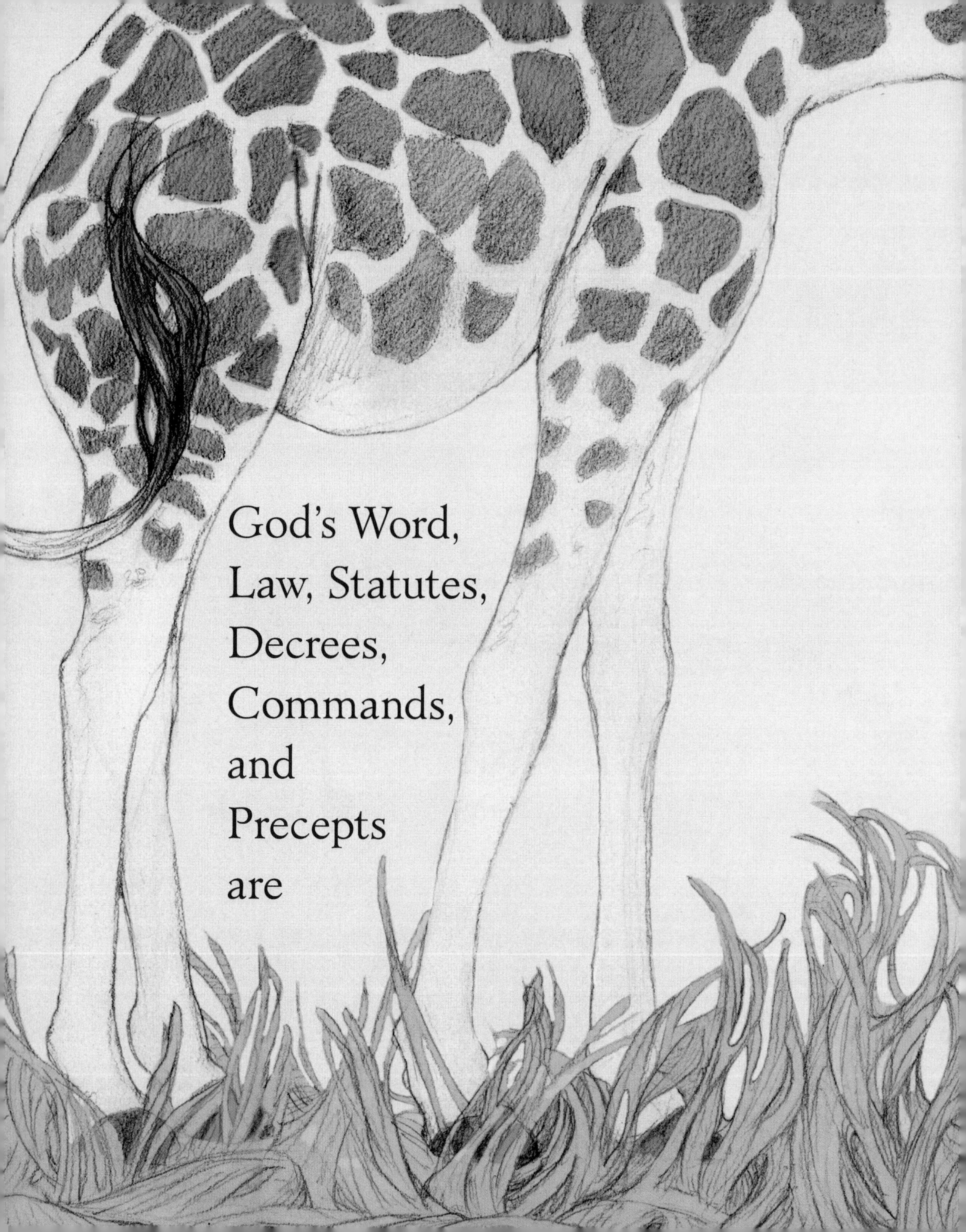

God's Word,
Law, Statutes,
Decrees,
Commands,
and
Precepts
are

G
good

God's Word, Law, Statutes, Decrees, Commands, and Precepts are

H
helpful

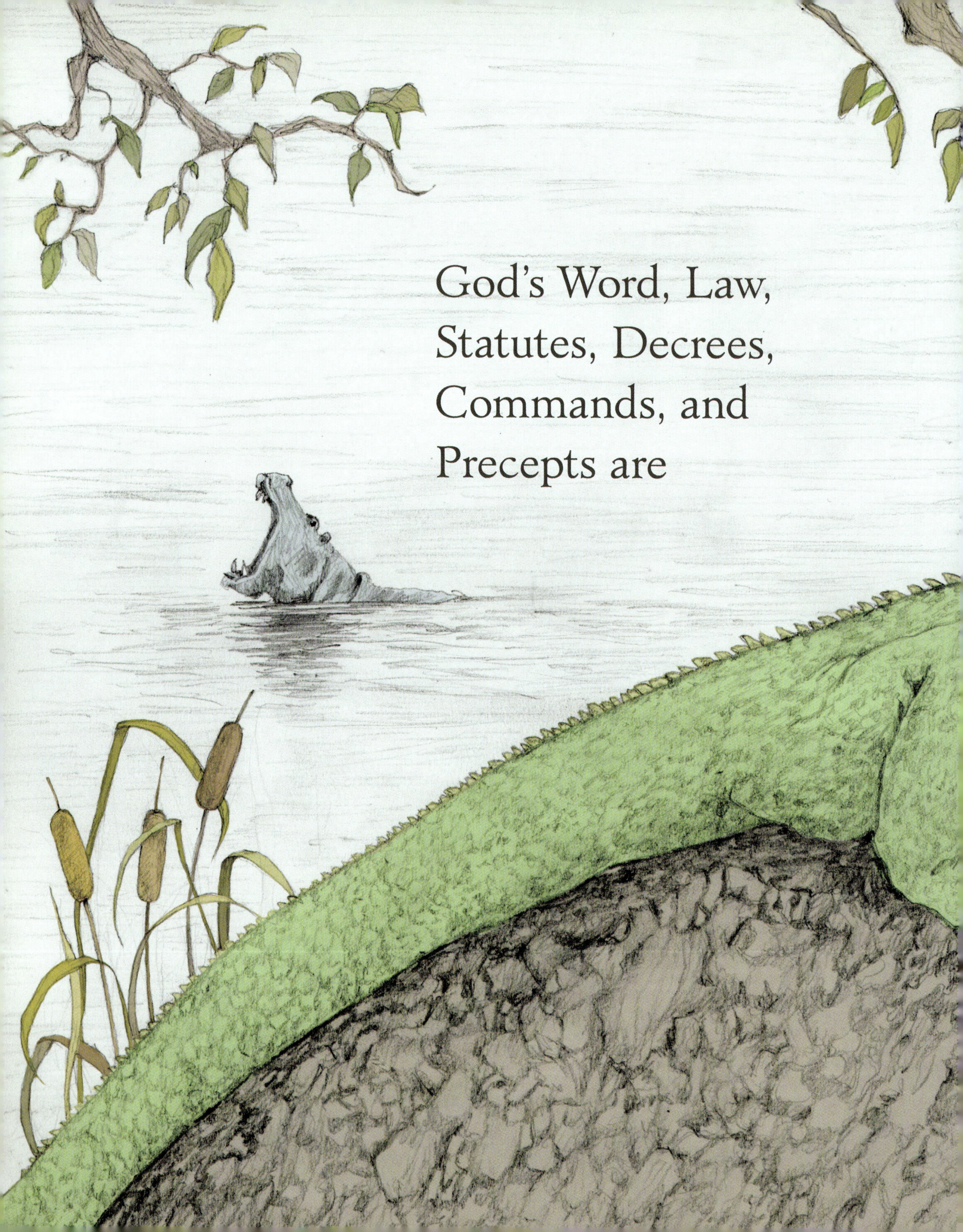

God's Word, Law, Statutes, Decrees, Commands, and Precepts are

I
instructive

God's Word, Law, Statutes, Decrees, Commands, and Precepts are

J
just

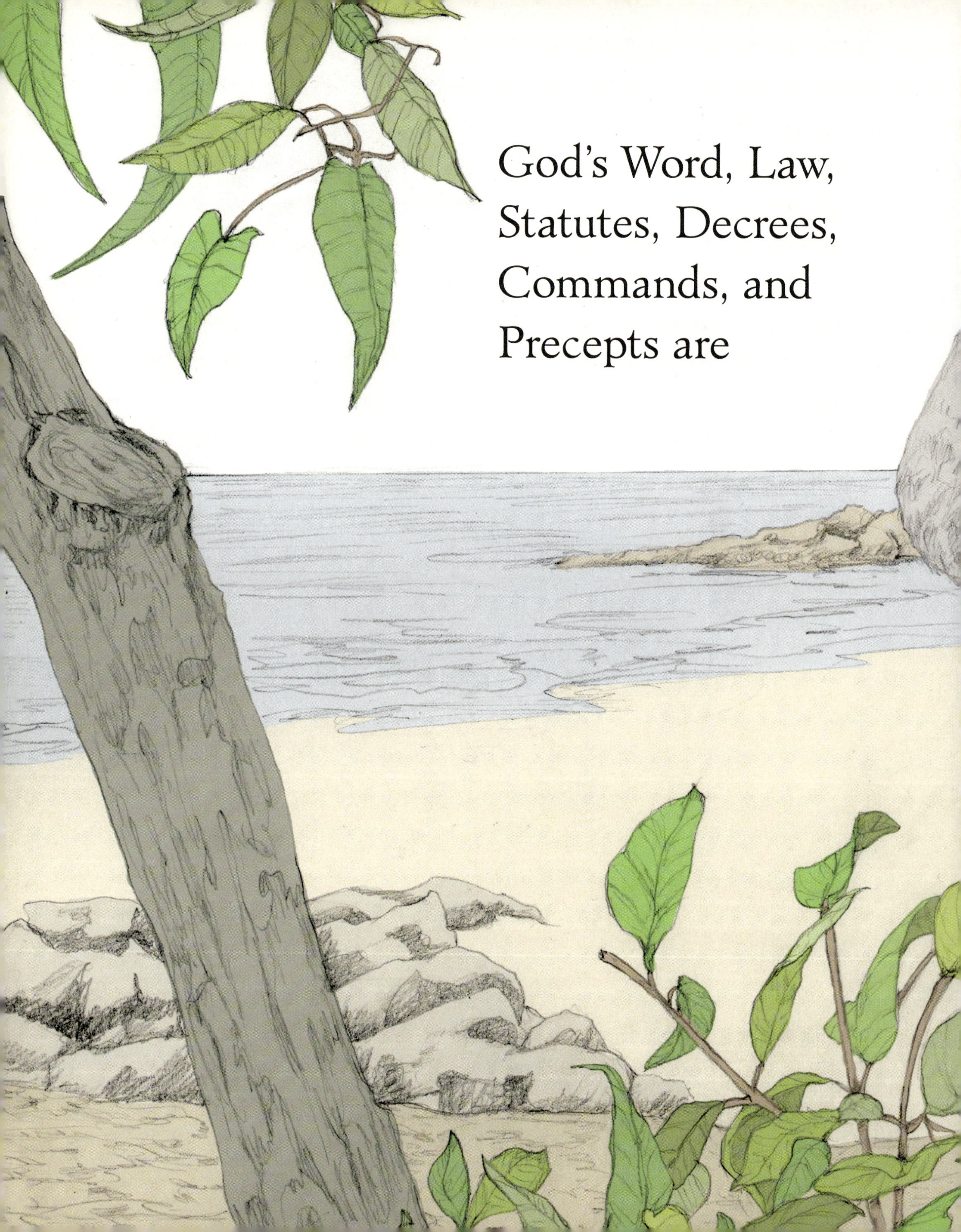

God's Word, Law, Statutes, Decrees, Commands, and Precepts are

K
kind

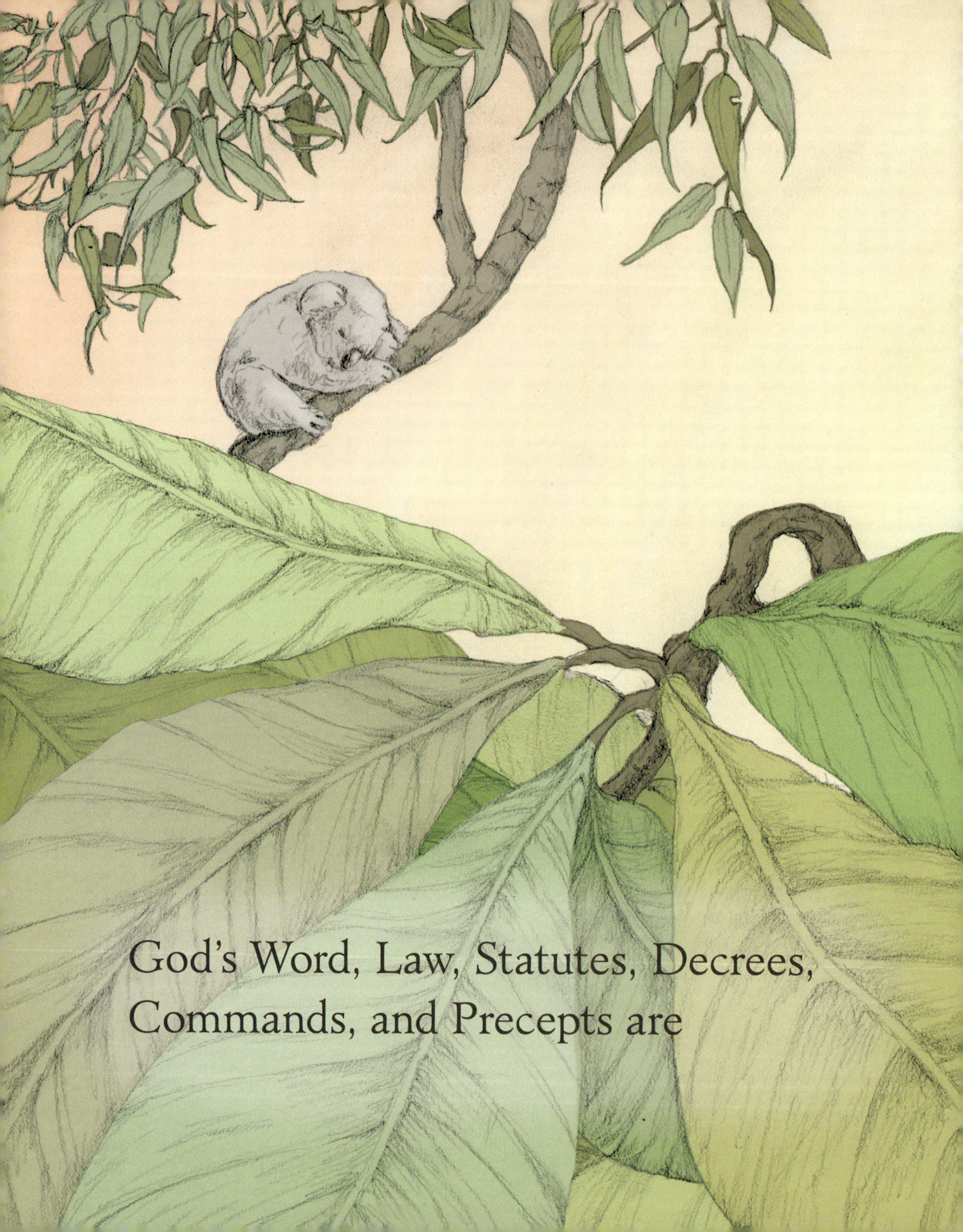

God's Word, Law, Statutes, Decrees, Commands, and Precepts are

L
light

God's Word, Law, Statutes, Decrees, Commands, and Precepts are

M
merciful

God's Word, Law, Statutes, Decrees, Commands, and Precepts are

N
near

God's Word, Law, Statutes, Decrees, Commands, and Precepts are

O
orderly

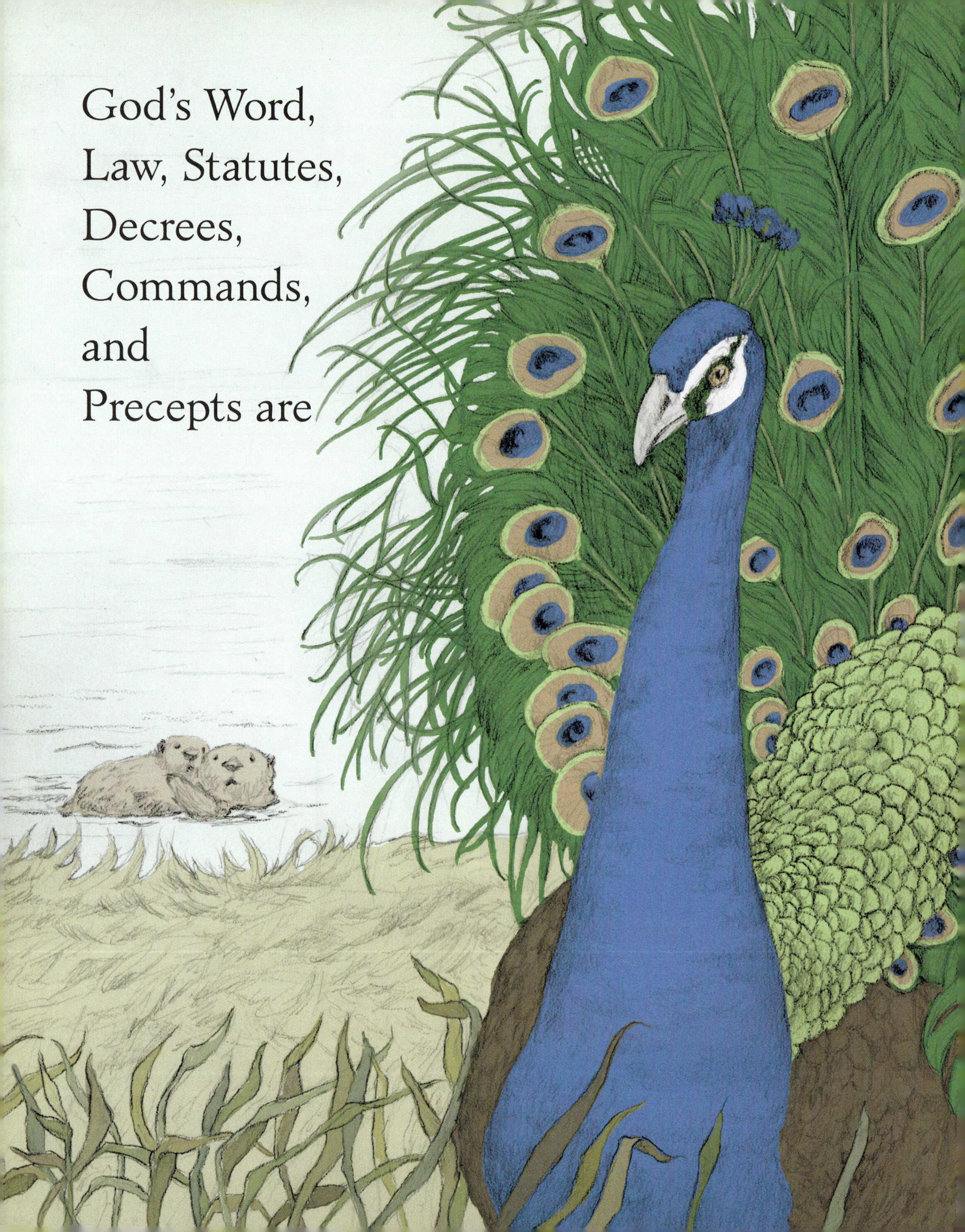

God's Word,
Law, Statutes,
Decrees,
Commands,
and
Precepts are

P
perfect

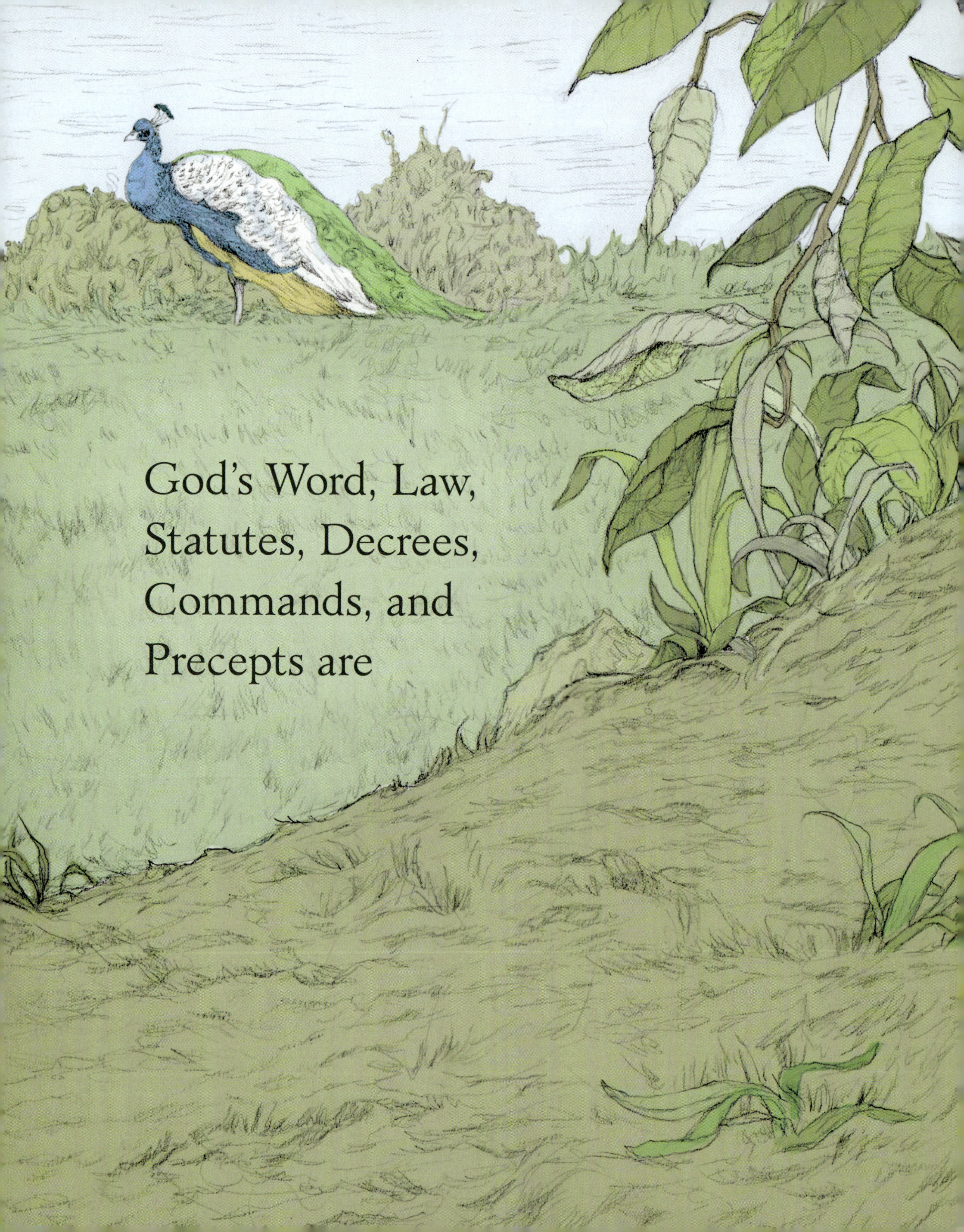

God's Word, Law,
Statutes, Decrees,
Commands, and
Precepts are

Q
quieting

God's Word, Law, Statutes, Decrees,
Commands, and Precepts are

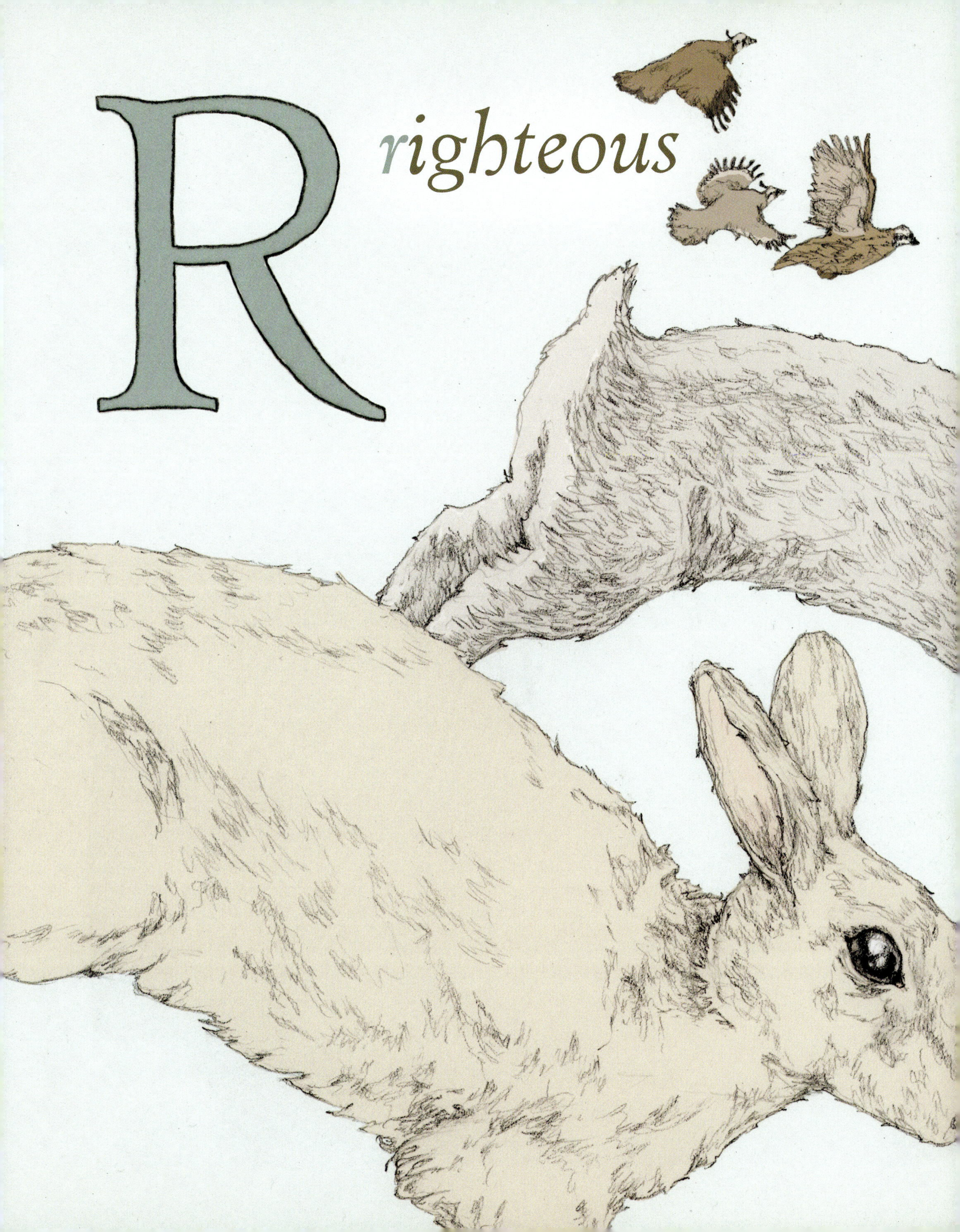
R
righteous

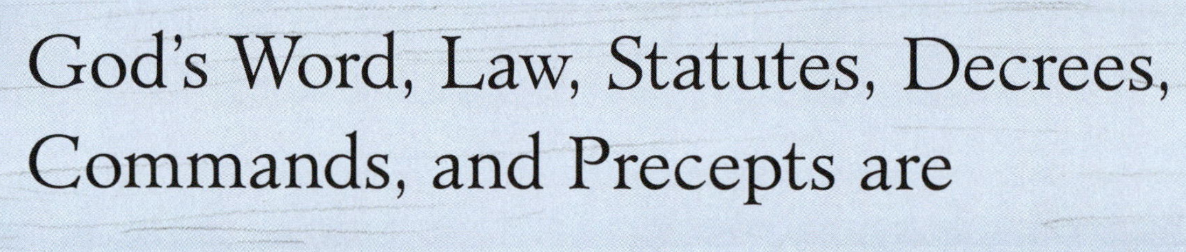

God's Word, Law, Statutes, Decrees, Commands, and Precepts are

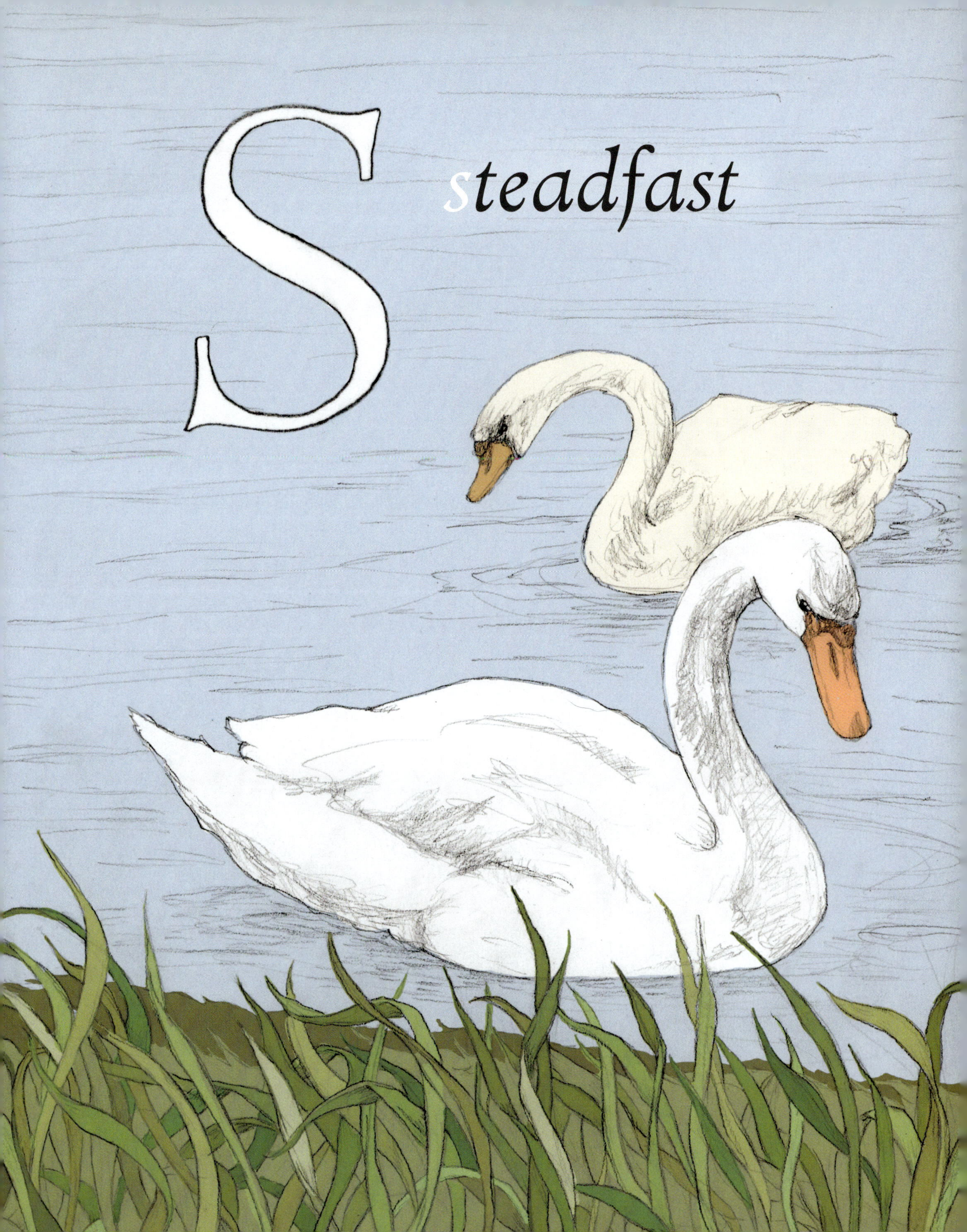
S
steadfast

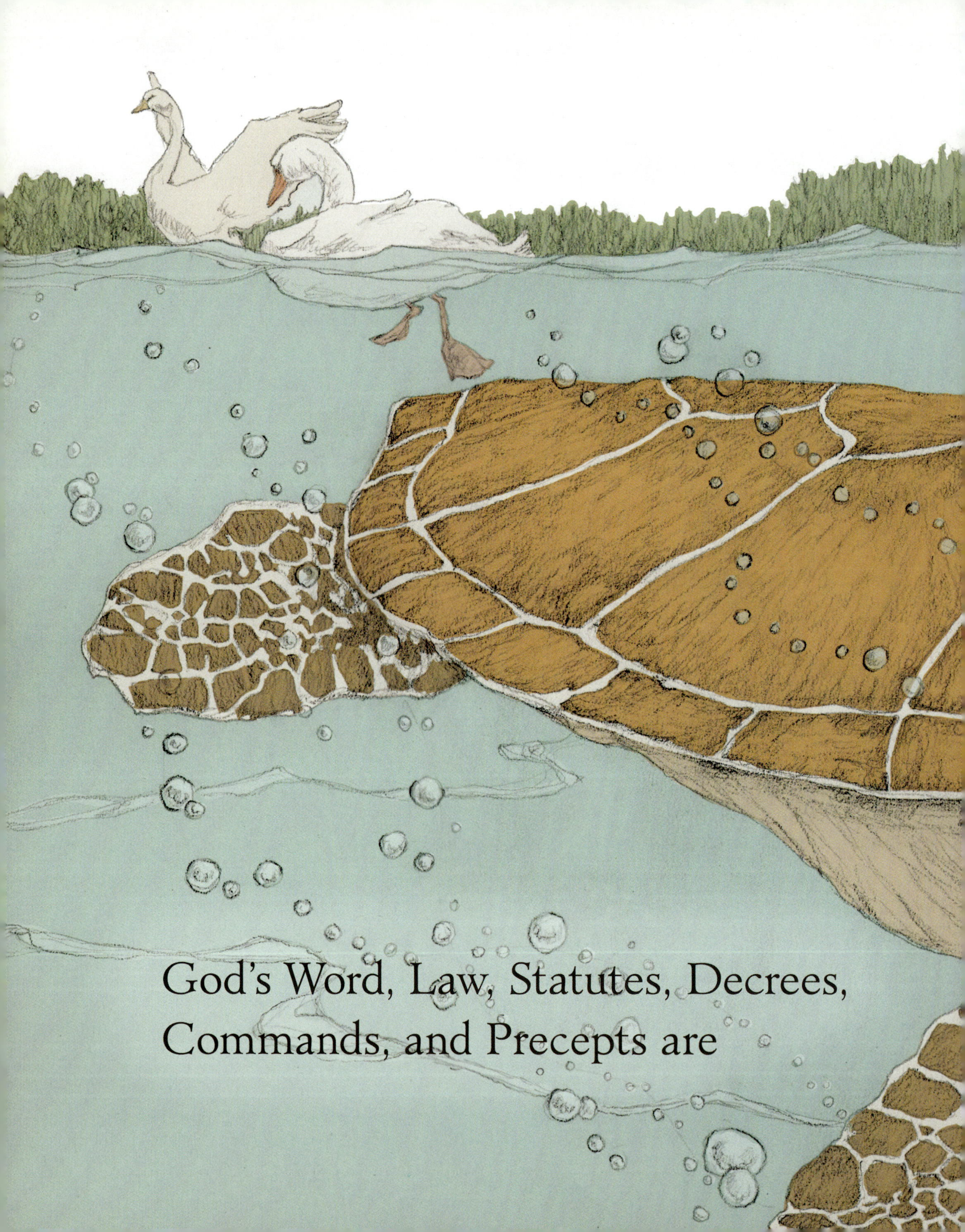

God's Word, Law, Statutes, Decrees,
Commands, and Precepts are

T
true

God's Word, Law, Statutes, Decrees, Commands, and Precepts are

U
universal

God's Word, Law, Statutes, Decrees,
Commands, and Precepts are

V
valuable

God's Word, Law, Statutes, Decrees, Commands, and Precepts are

W
wonderful

God's Word, Law, Statutes, Decrees, Commands, and Precepts are

X
excellent

God's Word, Law,
Statutes, Decrees,
Commands, and
Precepts are

Y
year-
round

God's Word, Law,
Statutes, Decrees,
Commands, and
Precepts are

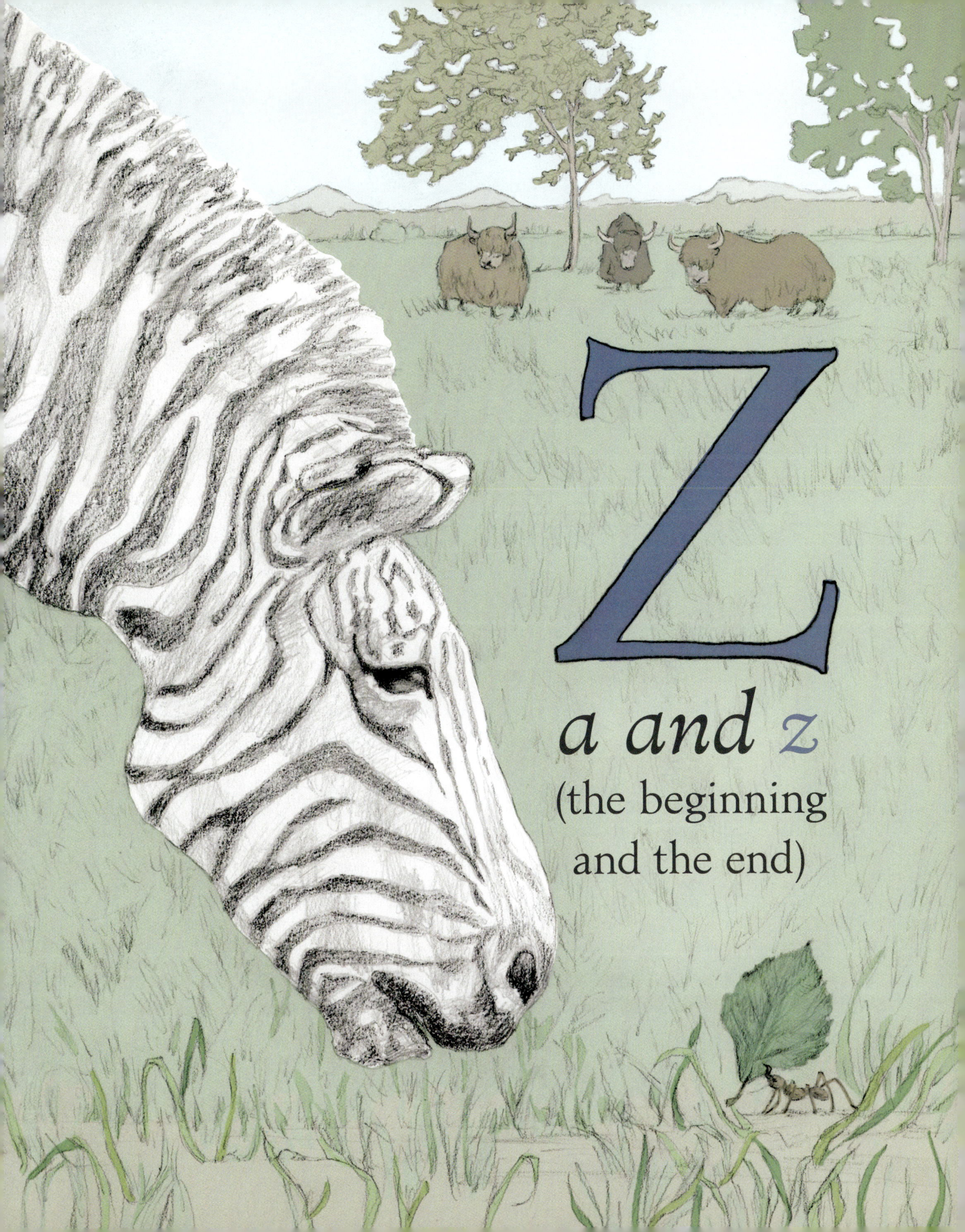
Z
a and z
(the beginning
and the end)

[1] Blessed are they whose ways are blameless,
who walk according to the law of the Lord.
[2] Blessed are they who keep his statutes
and seek him with all their heart.
[3] They do nothing wrong;
they walk in his ways.
[4] You have laid down precepts
that are to be fully obeyed.
[5] Oh, that my ways were steadfast
in obeying your decrees!
[6] Then I would not be put to shame
when I consider all your commands.
[7] I will praise you with an upright heart
as I learn your righteous laws.
[8] I will obey your decrees;
do not utterly forsake me.

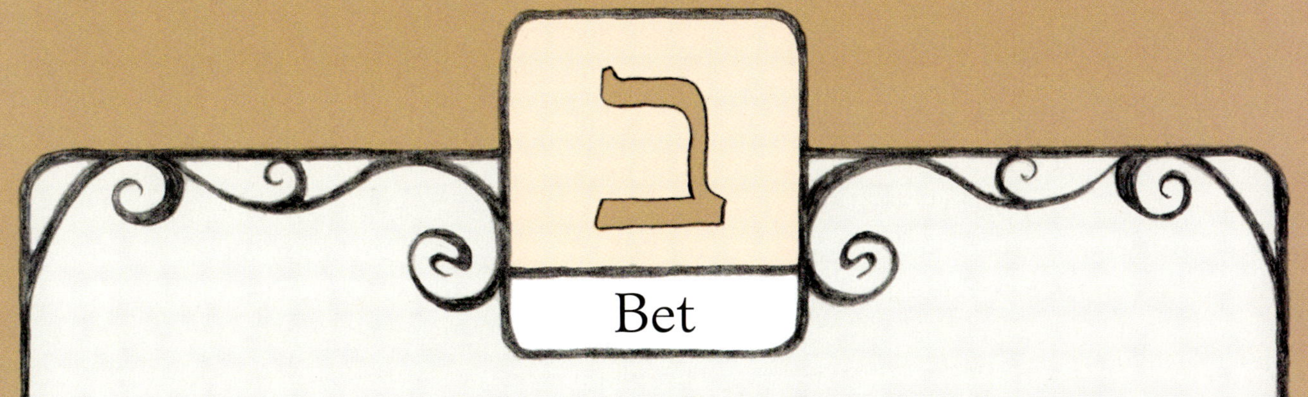

9 How can a young man keep his way pure?
By living according to your word.
10 I seek you with all my heart;
do not let me stray from your commands.
11 I have hidden your word in my heart
that I might not sin against you.
12 Praise be to you, O Lord;
teach me your decrees.
13 With my lips I recount
all the laws that come from your mouth.
14 I rejoice in following your statutes
as one rejoices in great riches.
15 I meditate on your precepts
and consider your ways.
16 I delight in your decrees;
I will not neglect your word.

[17] Do good to your servant, and I will live;
I will obey your word.
[18] Open my eyes that I may see
wonderful things in your law.
[19] I am a stranger on earth;
do not hide your commands from me.
[20] My soul is consumed with longing
for your laws at all times.
[21] You rebuke the arrogant, who are cursed
and who stray from your commands.
[22] Remove from me scorn and contempt,
for I keep your statutes.
[23] Though rulers sit together and slander me,
your servant will meditate on your decrees.
[24] Your statutes are my delight;
they are my counselors.

25 I am laid low in the dust;
preserve my life according to your word.
26 I recounted my ways and you answered me;
teach me your decrees.
27 Let me understand the teaching of your precepts;
then I will meditate on your wonders.
28 My soul is weary with sorrow;
strengthen me according to your word.
29 Keep me from deceitful ways;
be gracious to me through your law.
30 I have chosen the way of truth;
I have set my heart on your laws.
31 I hold fast to your statutes, O Lord;
do not let me be put to shame.
32 I run in the path of your commands,
for you have set my heart free.

33 Teach me, O Lord, to follow your decrees;
then I will keep them to the end.
34 Give me understanding, and I will keep your law
and obey it with all my heart.
35 Direct me in the path of your commands,
for there I find delight.
36 Turn my heart toward your statutes
and not toward selfish gain.
37 Turn my eyes away from worthless things;
preserve my life according to your word.
38 Fulfill your promise to your servant,
so that you may be feared.
39 Take away the disgrace I dread,
for your laws are good.
40 How I long for your precepts!
Preserve my life in your righteousness.

41 May your unfailing love come to me, O Lord,
your salvation according to your promise;
42 then I will answer the one who taunts me,
for I trust in your word.
43 Do not snatch the word of truth from my mouth,
for I have put my hope in your laws.
44 I will always obey your law,
for ever and ever.
45 I will walk about in freedom,
for I have sought out your precepts.
46 I will speak of your statutes before kings
and will not be put to shame,
47 for I delight in your commands
because I love them.
48 I lift up my hands to your commands, which I love,
and I meditate on your decrees.

49 Remember your word to your servant,
for you have given me hope.
50 My comfort in my suffering is this:
Your promise preserves my life.
51 The arrogant mock me without restraint,
but I do not turn from your law.
52 I remember your ancient laws, O Lord,
and I find comfort in them.
53 Indignation grips me because of the wicked,
who have forsaken your law.
54 Your decrees are the theme of my song
wherever I lodge.
55 In the night I remember your name, O Lord,
and I will keep your law.
56 This has been my practice:
I obey your precepts.

57 You are my portion, O Lord;
I have promised to obey your words.
58 I have sought your face with all my heart;
be gracious to me according to your promise.
59 I have considered my ways
and have turned my steps to your statutes.
60 I will hasten and not delay
to obey your commands.
61 Though the wicked bind me with ropes,
I will not forget your law.
62 At midnight I rise to give you thanks
for your righteous laws.
63 I am a friend to all who fear you,
to all who follow your precepts.
64 The earth is filled with your love, O Lord;
teach me your decrees.

[65] Do good to your servant
according to your word, O Lord.
[66] Teach me knowledge and good judgment,
for I believe in your commands.
[67] Before I was afflicted I went astray,
but now I obey your word.
[68] You are good, and what you do is good;
teach me your decrees.
[69] Though the arrogant have smeared me with lies,
I keep your precepts with all my heart.
[70] Their hearts are callous and unfeeling,
but I delight in your law.
[71] It was good for me to be afflicted
so that I might learn your decrees.
[72] The law from your mouth is more precious to me
than thousands of pieces of silver and gold.

[73] Your hands made me and formed me;
give me understanding to learn your commands.
[74] May those who fear you rejoice when they see me,
for I have put my hope in your word.
[75] I know, O Lord, that your laws are righteous,
and in faithfulness you have afflicted me.
[76] May your unfailing love be my comfort,
according to your promise to your servant.
[77] Let your compassion come to me that I may live,
for your law is my delight.
[78] May the arrogant be put to shame for wronging me
without cause;
but I will meditate on your precepts.
[79] May those who fear you turn to me,
those who understand your statutes.
[80] May my heart be blameless toward your decrees,
that I may not be put to shame.

81 My soul faints with longing for your salvation,
but I have put my hope in your word.
82 My eyes fail, looking for your promise;
I say, "When will you comfort me?"
83 Though I am like a wineskin in the smoke,
I do not forget your decrees.
84 How long must your servant wait?
When will you punish my persecutors?
85 The arrogant dig pitfalls for me,
contrary to your law.
86 All your commands are trustworthy;
help me, for men persecute me without cause.
87 They almost wiped me from the earth,
but I have not forsaken your precepts.
88 Preserve my life according to your love,
and I will obey the statutes of your mouth.

89 Your word, O Lord, is eternal;
it stands firm in the heavens.
90 Your faithfulness continues through all generations;
you established the earth, and it endures.
91 Your laws endure to this day,
for all things serve you.
92 If your law had not been my delight,
I would have perished in my affliction.
93 I will never forget your precepts,
for by them you have preserved my life.
94 Save me, for I am yours;
I have sought out your precepts.
95 The wicked are waiting to destroy me,
but I will ponder your statutes.
96 To all perfection I see a limit;
but your commands are boundless.

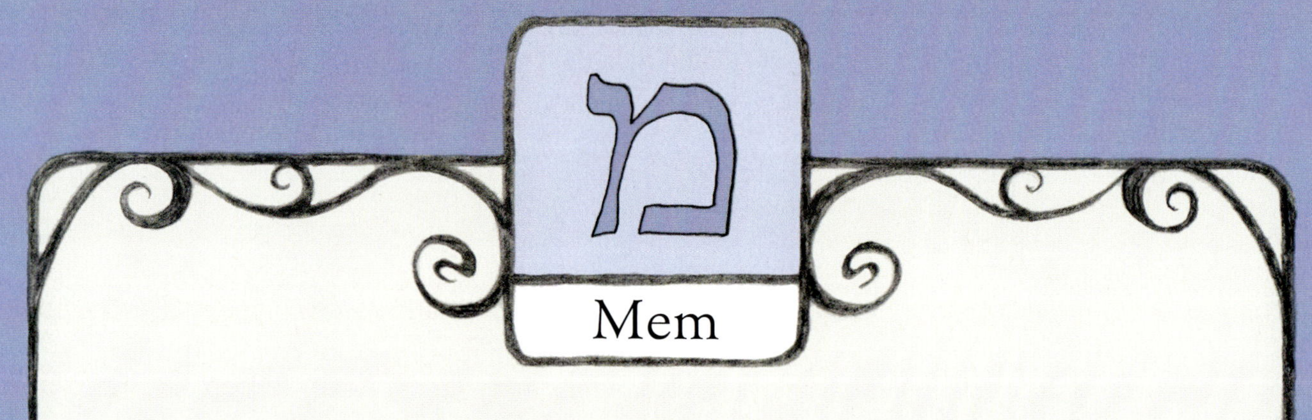

97 Oh, how I love your law!
I meditate on it all day long.
98 Your commands make me wiser than my enemies,
for they are ever with me.
99 I have more insight than all my teachers,
for I meditate on your statutes.
100 I have more understanding than the elders,
for I obey your precepts.
101 I have kept my feet from every evil path
so that I might obey your word.
102 I have not departed from your laws,
for you yourself have taught me.
103 How sweet are your words to my taste,
sweeter than honey to my mouth!
104 I gain understanding from your precepts;
therefore I hate every wrong path.

105 Your word is a lamp to my feet
and a light for my path.
106 I have taken an oath and confirmed it,
that I will follow your righteous laws.
107 I have suffered much;
preserve my life, O Lord, according to your word.
108 Accept, O Lord, the willing praise of my mouth,
and teach me your laws.
109 Though I constantly take my life in my hands,
I will not forget your law.
110 The wicked have set a snare for me,
but I have not strayed from your precepts.
111 Your statutes are my heritage forever;
they are the joy of my heart.
112 My heart is set on keeping your decrees
to the very end.

113 I hate double-minded men,
but I love your law.
114 You are my refuge and my shield;
I have put my hope in your word.
115 Away from me, you evildoers,
that I may keep the commands of my God!
116 Sustain me according to your promise, and I will live;
do not let my hopes be dashed.
117 Uphold me, and I will be delivered;
I will always have regard for your decrees.
118 You reject all who stray from your decrees,
for their deceitfulness is in vain.
119 All the wicked of the earth you discard like dross;
therefore I love your statutes.
120 My flesh trembles in fear of you;
I stand in awe of your laws.

121 I have done what is righteous and just;
do not leave me to my oppressors.
122 Ensure your servant's well-being;
let not the arrogant oppress me.
123 My eyes fail, looking for your salvation,
looking for your righteous promise.
124 Deal with your servant according to your love
and teach me your decrees.
125 I am your servant; give me discernment
that I may understand your statutes.
126 It is time for you to act, O Lord;
your law is being broken.
127 Because I love your commands
more than gold, more than pure gold,
128 and because I consider all your precepts right,
I hate every wrong path.

129 Your statutes are wonderful;
therefore I obey them.
130 The unfolding of your words gives light;
it gives understanding to the simple.
131 I open my mouth and pant,
longing for your commands.
132 Turn to me and have mercy on me,
as you always do to those who love your name.
133 Direct my footsteps according to your word;
let no sin rule over me.
134 Redeem me from the oppression of men,
that I may obey your precepts.
135 Make your face shine upon your servant
and teach me your decrees.
136 Streams of tears flow from my eyes,
for your law is not obeyed.

137 Righteous are you, O Lord,
and your laws are right.
138 The statutes you have laid down are righteous;
they are fully trustworthy.
139 My zeal wears me out,
for my enemies ignore your words.
140 Your promises have been thoroughly tested,
and your servant loves them.
141 Though I am lowly and despised,
I do not forget your precepts.
142 Your righteousness is everlasting
and your law is true.
143 Trouble and distress have come upon me,
but your commands are my delight.
144 Your statutes are forever right;
give me understanding that I may live.

Qof

145 I call with all my heart; answer me, O Lord,
and I will obey your decrees.
146 I call out to you; save me
and I will keep your statutes.
147 I rise before dawn and cry for help;
I have put my hope in your word.
148 My eyes stay open through the watches of the night,
that I may meditate on your promises.
149 Hear my voice in accordance with your love;
preserve my life, O Lord, according to your laws.
150 Those who devise wicked schemes are near,
but they are far from your law.
151 Yet you are near, O Lord,
and all your commands are true.
152 Long ago I learned from your statutes
that you established them to last forever.

153 Look upon my suffering and deliver me,
for I have not forgotten your law.
154 Defend my cause and redeem me;
preserve my life according to your promise.
155 Salvation is far from the wicked,
for they do not seek out your decrees.
156 Your compassion is great, O Lord;
preserve my life according to your laws.
157 Many are the foes who persecute me,
but I have not turned from your statutes.
158 I look on the faithless with loathing,
for they do not obey your word.
159 See how I love your precepts;
preserve my life, O Lord, according to your love.
160 All your words are true;
all your righteous laws are eternal.

161 Rulers persecute me without cause,
but my heart trembles at your word.
162 I rejoice in your promise
like one who finds great spoil.
163 I hate and abhor falsehood
but I love your law.
164 Seven times a day I praise you
for your righteous laws.
165 Great peace have they who love your law,
and nothing can make them stumble.
166 I wait for your salvation, O Lord,
and I follow your commands.
167 I obey your statutes,
for I love them greatly.
168 I obey your precepts and your statutes,
for all my ways are known to you.

169 May my cry come before you, O Lord;
give me understanding according to your word.
170 May my supplication come before you;
deliver me according to your promise.
171 May my lips overflow with praise,
for you teach me your decrees.
172 May my tongue sing of your word,
for all your commands are righteous.
173 May your hand be ready to help me,
for I have chosen your precepts.
174 I long for your salvation, O Lord,
and your law is my delight.
175 Let me live that I may praise you,
and may your laws sustain me.
176 I have strayed like a lost sheep.
Seek your servant,
for I have not forgotten your commands.

Also written by Davis Carman
and illustrated by Alice Ratterree:

Good Morning, God